MW01518164

MAR 0 1 2021

JULIE ERTZ

Kerrily Sapet

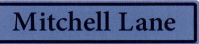

PUBLISHERS

mitchelllane.com

2001 SW 31st Avenue
Hallandale, FL 33009

First Edition, 2021.
Author: Kerrily Sapet
Designer: Ed Morgan
Editor: Morgan Brody

Series: Blue Banner Biographies
Title: Julie Ertz / by Kerrily Sapet

Hallandale, FL : Mitchell Lane Publishers, [2021]

Library bound ISBN: 978-1-68020-625-8
eBook ISBN: 978-1-68020-626-5

PHOTO CREDITS: Design Elements, freepik.com, cover: Andrew Bershaw/Icon Sportswire DJR/Andrew Bershaw/Icon Sportswire/ Newscom, p. 5 Brad Smith/ZUMA Press/Newscom, p. 7 Dylan Stewart/Image of Sport/Newscom, p. 9 Ricky Fitchett/ZUMA Press/ Newscom, p. 11 Chris Szagola/Cal Sport Media/Newscom, p. 13 Daniel Bartel/ZUMA Press/Newscom, p. 15 De .CC0 1.0, p. 17 Brad Smith/ZUMA Press/Newscom, p. 19 Noah Salzman CC-BY-SA-4.0, p. 21 Andrew Chin/ZUMA Press/Newscom, p. 23 Agência Brasília CC-BY-2.0, p. 24 Chris Williams/Icon Sportswire 007/Chris Williams/Icon Sportswire/Newscom, p. 26 Daniel Bartel/ZUMA Press/ Newscom

Contents

Olympic Dreams

WHEN JULIE ERTZ was a young girl, she loved the Olympics. She and her family sat around the television and watched as the world's best athletes competed. Her parents told stories about legendary Olympians. Julie stayed up as late as she could, glued to the flickering images on television, and often fell asleep on the couch. As Julie watched, she imagined she was there and part of the excitement. "I think every kid who has watched the Olympics has, at some point, dreamed of becoming an Olympian," Julie said. "I was no different."

Julie Ertz (*left*) chats with Brandi Chastain and Sofia Huerta before a match in July 2017.

Julie's favorite sport to watch was soccer. She had been playing soccer since she was four years old. When the U.S. Women's National Soccer Team won the gold medal in 2004, Julie was one of the millions of TV viewers watching. After the Olympics, the team went on tour, playing games around the United States. Julie went to their game in Phoenix, Arizona, an hour away from her home. She watched her heroes, Mia Hamm and Brandi Chastain, and cheered until her throat was hoarse. After the game, she waited in a long line to get Brandi Chastain's autograph.

Growing up, Julie often felt different from other girls because she was athletic. She even tried to hide her muscles sometimes. After seeing talented, tough female soccer players in action though, Julie wanted to be like them. ". . . The second I put on my soccer outfit, I didn't care what I looked like," she said. "I wanted to win. I wanted to play."

Over the next ten years, Julie competed in hundreds of games. She practiced dribbling, kicking, passing, and shooting for thousands of hours. Julie pushed herself to become stronger and faster. Her dedication and focus would help her to become one of the best soccer players in the world, competing in the Olympics, and winning two World Cup titles. Today, Julie Ertz is a soccer legend and young fans wait in line to get *her* autograph.

Ertz is known for being a tough competitor whether she's practicing or playing a match.

The Mountain

JULIE BETH JOHNSON was born on August 6, 1992 in Mesa, Arizona. Years later, she would change her last name to Ertz when she got married. Julie's father, David, worked at a food supply company, lifting heavy boxes of fresh and frozen foods all day. Her mother, Kristi, was a nurse. Julie had a sister, Melanie, who was two years older.

Julie's parents taught their daughters to work hard. They also encouraged them to try different sports. Julie was a natural athlete. At six months old, she could hang from the monkey bars at the playground. Julie tried swimming, t-ball, softball, basketball, and soccer.

Ertz's family helped her to become the world champion she is today.

When Julie first started playing soccer, she cried when she fell down. "If you're going to cry in this sport, it's not for you," her father said. Julie grew tougher and discovered she loved soccer. She was fast on the field and fiercely competitive. When Julie was eight years old, she joined the Arizona Arsenal Soccer Club. Julie practiced during the week and played games on the weekends. "She would learn a move and practice that move over and over until she had it," said her coach, Dan Wolf.

Julie's parents helped her practice. They turned her chores into races and held a stick for her to jump over as she ran circles on their trampoline. Julie challenged herself by running up a nearby mountain. Even her dog wouldn't run with her because of the prickly desert cacti.

When Julie's third grade teacher asked the class to draw what they wanted to be when they grew up, Julie drew a soccer player. "I played soccer because I loved it so much," she said. "I felt most like myself when I was out on the field with a ball at my feet." When Julie was twelve years old, her parents suggested she try out for a team that would challenge her more. Julie dreaded being the new kid on the team, but she wanted to improve.

Julie started playing for Sereno Soccer Club, one of the best teams in Arizona. Her parents worked extra shifts to cover the cost. The family drove hours to and from practices, bringing frozen bottles of Gatorade to beat the blazing Arizona heat, and eating pizza dinners in the car. Julie quickly improved. Her new teammates nicknamed her "Jules" and "J.J."

Julie played for Sereno Soccer Club until she graduated from high school in 2010. Her team won the state championship nine times. Julie also attended camps and played on U.S. national teams for young players. After high school, Julie decided to attend Santa Clara University in California. She felt ready to tackle a new soccer challenge.

Fans often recognize Ertz on the field by the baby blue headband she wears during every match.

Training to Win

JULIE ERTZ chose Santa Clara University, in Santa Clara, California, because it had one of the top soccer programs in the country. The team's coach, Jerry Smith, had coached future Olympic gold medalists, such as Aly Wagner and Brandi Chastain. Julie split her time between training, playing games, and attending classes.

The love of soccer has helped Ertz overcome tough times and challenges in her life.

Santa Clara University was 700 miles away from home. Ertz missed her family and friends. Playing soccer helped her feel less lonely. "If I'm sad, I go kick a soccer ball," Ertz said. "If I'm stressed, I go and kick a soccer ball. If I'm in a good mood, I go kick a soccer ball . . . I just do it because it's something I love to do."

Ertz played as a defender on the field, blocking the other team from passing, shooting, and scoring. In her first year on the Santa Clara Broncos, Ertz played in 20 games and was named the West Coast Conference Freshman of the Year. She only got better. In her junior year, she scored eight goals and was the team's leading scorer.

Ertz played soccer throughout the year. In the fall and winter, she played for her college team. In the spring and summer, she attended training camps and played for youth national teams. In 2012, Ertz helped the U-20 national team (for players under 20 years old) win the U-20 World Cup. She was named the U.S. Soccer Young Female Player of the Year.

By the time Ertz graduated, she had played in 79 games and scored 31 goals for her college team. She also had won multiple awards. Ertz dreamed of earning a spot on the full women's national team and playing for the United States at the Olympic Games and in World Cup tournaments. "The value of the dream wasn't in whether it was going to come true," she said. "It was in the hope and drive it gave me to persist through the tough times." In January 2013, Ertz's years of hard work and dedication paid off and she was named to the full women's national team. Her soccer career was about to begin.

World Cup Japan 2012

Ertz proudly holds her trophies high after winning the
U-20 World Cup in Japan.

Overcoming Defeat

JULIE ERTZ played her first match for the U.S. Women's National Team on February 9, 2013. It was her first "cap"—a term for playing a game with a national team. She helped the team defeat Scotland. It would be one of many "caps" during her career.

When Ertz wasn't playing for the national team, she played for the Chicago Red Stars, a professional soccer team. In her debut game, against the Western New York Flash, she scored the game-winning goal. That year she played in 21 games and scored two goals.

Ertz gets ready to attack the ball as it comes in her direction at practice.

Ertz hoped to be one of the members of the national team competing at the 2015 World Cup. She started practicing with Carli Lloyd, another player on the team, and Lloyd's trainer, James Galanis. Ertz trained for three hours, twice a day. She ran, passed, and worked on her foot skills. She practiced throughout the snowy winter and rainy spring.

Ertz was driving in the car with her sister when she got a phone call that changed her life. Crystal Dunn, a player on the team, was injured and couldn't compete in the World Cup. Ertz would get to take her spot on the team!

Ertz wasn't famous when she played her first World Cup match, but soon fans were cheering her name. She played in every minute of every game as the U.S. team advanced. Ertz fearlessly defended the net and shot spectacular goals. "I always call J.J. my warrior," said Jill Ellis, the team's coach.

Ertz shows focus, balance, and strength as she lunges towards the ball during a match in May 2015.

On July 5, 2015, the team defeated Japan to win the World Cup. "It was an amazing moment," Ertz said. "It was a cool cherry on top of the cake for the whole year and the journey to the World Cup."

When the team returned to the United States, a parade was held in their honor in New York City. They rode on floats as colorful confetti rained down, tossed from the windows of tall buildings. Ertz loved seeing all the young girls, inspired to become athletes, cheering for them.

When the celebrations ended, Ertz started training for the 2016 Olympics that would be held in Rio de Janeiro, Brazil. "I want to win more games," she said. "It's such an honor to represent your country that I don't ever want to let it down." But Ertz would soon face the most difficult year of her career.

The U.S. Women's National Team celebrates their World Cup victory against Japan in 2015.

A World Champion

JULIE ERTZ had always dreamed of being an Olympic athlete. Now she was on the U.S. Women's National Team competing in her first Olympics. Although everyone expected the U.S. team to win the gold medal, they didn't win any medal. They lost to Sweden in the quarterfinal match. "It's one of those games that leaves a bad taste in your mouth and it's a feeling you don't ever want to experience again," Ertz said.

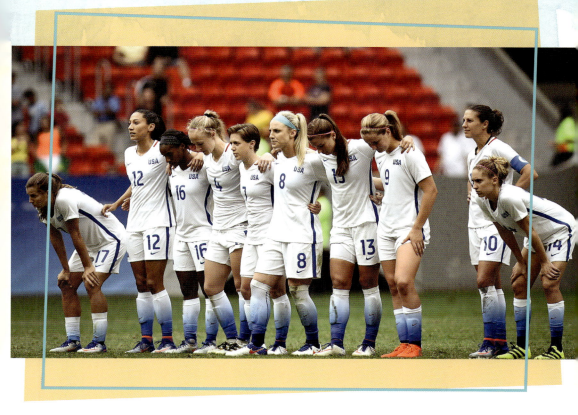

In 2016, Ertz and the national team faced a tough loss to Sweden at the Olympics.

For Ertz, the Olympic defeat was heartbreaking. Even worse, she lost her spot on the team when Coach Jill Ellis named another player to Ertz's position. Ertz thought about retiring. Instead, she decided to fight for her spot by training even harder.

Ertz scores the game-winning goal at the Tournament of Nations match against Brazil in 2017.

Ertz got her chance in July 2017 when Coach Ellis asked her to be a substitute in a game. Ellis wanted her to play as a midfielder instead of a defender. Ertz would need to pass, win headers (hitting the ball with her head to pass or shoot it), and score goals. It was a big change, but Ertz was excited to play. During the game, she hammered the ball into the net to score the game-winning goal. Ertz scored five goals in the next seven games and was named the U.S. Soccer Women's Player of the Year.

In 2017, she married Zach Ertz, a professional football player with the Philadelphia Eagles. Both successful athletes, they want to use their fame and fortune to help others. Together they started a charity, the Ertz Family Foundation, to help children in need. They donate backpacks filled with school supplies and provide Thanksgiving meals to families. Ertz also runs youth soccer camps. "Believe in yourself so much that other people can't help but believe in you too," she tells young players.

Ertz snaps a picture with young fans after a game.

In 2019, Julie Ertz competed in her second World Cup tournament. She helped the U.S. team defeat the Netherlands in the finals. When the team returned home, Ertz was the first one off the plane. She proudly held the trophy high for everyone to see.

Julie Ertz plans to be on the team going to the 2020 Olympics in Tokyo, Japan. Whether she wins a gold medal or not, Ertz is a champion. She tries to be her best on and off the field. She trains hard, follows her dreams, and helps others. She will be remembered as one of the greatest soccer players to step foot on the field.

Timeline

1992   Julie Ertz (Johnston) is born on April 6.

2004   Ertz starts playing with Sereno Soccer Club.

2010   Ertz attends Santa Clara University.

2012   Ertz is named U.S. Soccer's Young Female Player of the Year.

2013   Ertz begins playing for the women's national team.

2014   Ertz is drafted by the Chicago Red Stars.

2015   Ertz plays in her first World Cup.

2017   Ertz is named U.S. Soccer's Women's Player of the Year.

2019   Ertz helps her team win the World Cup.

Career Stats

U.S. Women's National Team
   Total games played   91
   Total goals scored   19
   Total assists   2
World Cup medals   **2 gold**
Chicago Red Stars
   Total games played   72
   Total goals scored   31

Find Out More

Books

Ignotofsky, Rachel. *Women in Sports: 50 Fearless Athletes Who Played to Win*. Berkeley, California, 2017.

Jokülsson, Illugi. *Stars of Women's Soccer*. New York, New York: Abbeville Kids, 2018.

Savage, Jeff. *U.S. Women's National Team: Soccer Champions*. Minneapolis, Minnesota, 2018.

On the Internet

Official Website of the Chicago Red Stars. http://chicagoredstars.com/julie-ertz/

Official U.S. Soccer Website. https://www.ussoccer.com/players/e/julie-ertz

Works Consulted

Baxter, Kevin. "Julie Johnston is Living Her Dream at Women's World Cup." *LA Times*, June 19, 2015. https://www.latimes.com/sports/soccer/la-sp-usa-soccer-johnston-20150620-story.html

Carver, Kristen. "World Cup Quest Began in Mesa for Women's National Team's Julie Johnston." *Cronkite News*, June 30, 2015. https://cronkitenews.azpbs.org/2015/06/30/johnstons-world-cup-quest-began-in-mesa/

Chow, Michael. "Julie Johnston's World Cup Journey Began in Mesa." *Fox Sports*, June 30, 2015. https://www.foxsports.com/arizona/story/julie-johnston-s-world-cup-journey-began-in-mesa-063015

Johnston, Julie. "Our Road to Rio." *The Players Tribune*, July 22, 2016. https://www.theplayerstribune.com/en-us/articles/julie-johnston-uswnt-soccer-olympics-rio

Litman, Laken. "Meet Julie Johnston: The Fringe Player Who Became the Spark of the U.S. Defense." *USA Today*, May 31, 2015. https://ftw.usatoday.com/2015/05/meet-julie-johnston-the-fringe-player-who-became-the-heart-of-the-u-s-defense

McCoy, Jenny. "How Olympian and Pro Soccer Player Julie Ertz Is Training for the 2019 Women's World Cup." *Self*, February 23, 2019. https://www.self.com/story/olympian-pro-soccer-player-julie-ertz-2019-womens-world-cup

Meraji, Shereen. "Julie Johnston: Player to Watch on U.S. Women's World Cup Team." *NPR*, June 8, 2015. https://www.npr.org/2015/06/08/412805157/julie-johnson-player-to-watch-on-the-u-s-women-s-world-cup-team

Petersen, Anne M. "Julie Ertz was Soccer Star Before Zach's Super Bowl Bid." *USA Today*, January 31, 2018. https://www.usatoday.com/story/sports/nfl/2018/01/31/julie-ertz-was-soccer-star-before-zachs-super-bowl-bid/109965362/

Studeman, Kristin. "2016 Summer Olympics: Soccer Fans, Look Out for Julie Johnston." *W. Magazine*, July 6, 2016. https://www.wmagazine.com/story/2016-summer-olympics-julie-johnston-soccer-interview

Taylor, Stephanie. "2017 is the 'Year of Ertz.'" *Girls Soccer Network*, February 1, 2018. https://girlssoccernetwork.com/profiles/2017-year-ertz/

Index

About the Author

Kerrily Sapet is the author of more than 30 children's books. She has written about queens, futuristic vehicles, sneakers, pioneers, and pyramids. Sapet has gone to a Chicago Fire soccer team game, spent hours at her son's soccer practices, and attended a stormy soccer tournament that ended with a tornado.